Farm Animals

Horses and Ponies

Camilla de la Bédoyère

QED

QED Publishing

Editor: Eve Marleau
Designer: Melissa Alaverdy
Picture Researcher: Maria Joannou

Copyright © QED Publishing 2010

First published in the UK in 2010 by
QED Publishing
A Quarto Group company
226 City Road
London EC1V 2TT

www.qed-publishing.co.uk

All rights reserved. No part of this publication
may be reproduced, stored in a retrieval system, or
transmitted in any form or by any means, electronic,
mechanical, photocopying, recording, or otherwise,
without the prior permission of the publisher, nor be
otherwise circulated in any form of binding or cover
other than that in which it is published and without
a similar condition being imposed on the subsequent
purchaser.

A catalogue record for this book is available
from the British Library.

ISBN 978 1 84835 447 0

Printed and bound in China

RENFREWSHIRE
COUNCIL

179637921

Bertrams	08/07/2011
	£4.99
CEN	

Words in **bold**
are explained in
the Glossary on
page 22.

Picture credits
(t=top, b=bottom, l=left, r=right, c=centre,
fc=front cover)

Alamy Images Wildlife GmbH 18tl;
Corbis Vladimir Godnik/Moodboard 15t;
Getty Images Taxi/Marsi 13t, Stone/Nicolas Russell
18-19; **Photolibrary** Imagebroker.net/Alessandra
Sarti 12t, Juniors Bildarchiv 12b, 22-23, Animals
Animals/Phil Degginger 12-13, Jörgen Brennicke
14-15, Alain Christof 16l, Y Arthus-Bertrand 21tr;
Shutterstock Harley Molesworth fcr, Janos Levente
fcl, Marilyn Barbone c, Eric Isselée 2t, Vhpfoto 2-3,
MisterElements 3, 5bl, 7b, 9b, 11bl, 13b, 14r, 17b, 18b,
21b, Postnikova Kristina 4-5, Zuzule 5t, 19tr, Karen
Givens 5c, Nikitin Anatoly Nikolaevich 5br, Dogist 6l,
Vicki France 6-7, Scott Sanders 8l, Stanislav Sokolov
8-9, Ivonne Wierink 9t, Stephanie Coffman 10-11,
Marekuliasz 11t, Elena Elisseeva 11br, Margo Harrison
14l, Karel Gallas 16r, D Kyslynskyy 17, Craig McAteer
20-21, Curtis Kautzer 24l, Abrakadabra 24 (icons),
ArttiC 24 (background).

Contents

What are horses and ponies?

Horses and ponies are large animals. They have four long legs with hooves. Each hoof is made of a hard, bony material.

Horses grow long, straight hair on their heads and necks. This hair is called a mane. It is the same colour as the horse's tail.

Horses and ponies can be different colours, such as brown or grey. Their fur may have **markings**, too.

tail

hoof

Horses and ponies are covered in fur. It helps them to stay warm.

A blaze is a wide marking on the face.

head

mane

A star is a white marking between the eyes.

A stripe is a thin marking on the face.

Farmyard Fact!

Very few horses and ponies have totally black fur. Most black horses have some white markings.

5

Horses and ponies on the farm

In the past, farmers used horses and ponies to pull heavy carts and ploughs.

Today, most farmers use machines, so horses and ponies are kept on farms for riding.

Farmers can measure how tall a horse is by using their hands. They measure from the ground to the withers, or shoulders.

⬆ One 'hand' is the width of an adult's hand (10 centimetres). This horse is 15 hands high.

Horses are more than 150 centimetres (15 hands) tall. Ponies are less than 147 centimetres (14.5 hands) tall.

horse

pony

Farmyard fact!

The smallest kind of pony is a Shetland pony. Many Shetlands are no more than one metre (10 hands) tall.

Where do horses and ponies live?

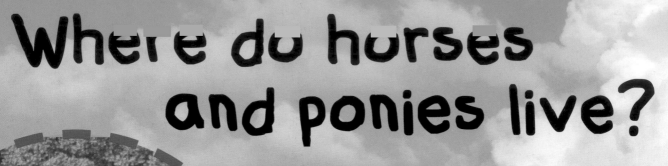

During the daytime, horses and ponies are kept in fields. They spend their time exercising and eat grass.

Farmers normally build shelters in the fields. The horses go to the shelters when they are too hot, too cold or too wet.

← A shelter protects the animals from the sun, rain and wind.

Horses and ponies ⇨ need plenty of space to exercise.

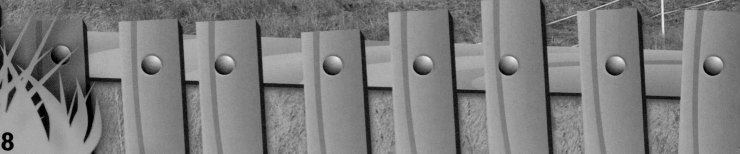

At the end of the day, farmers bring horses and ponies back from the fields and into stables for the night.

← The stables are warm and dry.

Farmyard Fact!

Stables need to be cleaned out every day. This is known as **mucking out**.

Whut do horses and ponies eat?

Horses and ponies mostly eat grass and hay. Farmers also give them water and some dry food.

Horses should not eat too much food at a time because it can make them ill. Sometimes, farmers give their horses and ponies a healthy treat. They love to eat apples and carrots.

Horses and ponies ⇨ **graze** on grass.

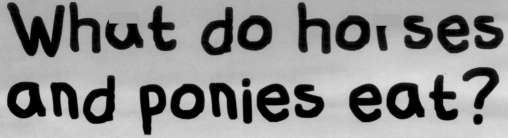

Dry food is called hard feed. Bran, oats, pony nuts and maize are types of hard feed.

⬆ Hard feed contains vitamins to keep horses healthy.

Hay is dried grass. ⮕ Horses also eat hay.

Farmyard Fact!

An average horse eats about 10 kilograms of food a day. That's the weight of 10 bags of sugar!

Looking after horses and ponies

Farmers ride their horses every day, or let them into a field. Horses like to walk around and graze on grass.

Horses need to be kept clean. Farmers groom, or brush, their horses and ponies to keep them healthy.

A **farrier** looks after the horses' hooves. They fit horses with shoes to stop their hooves cracking from walking on hard ground.

⇧ First, the farrier takes off the old horseshoe.

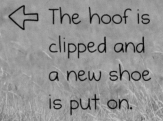

⇦ The hoof is clipped and a new shoe is put on.

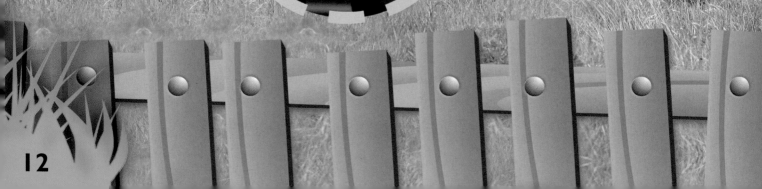

Tails and manes are brushed ⇨
to remove dirt, mud and hay.

⇩ In the wild, horses live
in groups called herds.

Farmyard Fact!

Farriers change horses'
shoes about eight times
every year. That's about
once every six weeks.

Riding horses and ponies

Most horses and ponies on farms are used for riding. Children usually ride ponies because ponies are smaller than horses.

Farmers also enter their horses and ponies into shows. They take part in competitions such as show jumping.

⇧ Most horses and ponies like to jump fences.

Farmyard Fact!

Horses and ponies are around five years old when they start taking part in competitions.

The tack room is where farmers keep the saddles and **bridles** that they use to ride horses and ponies.

Riders sit on saddles and use reins to control the horse or pony.

bridle

saddle

The life cycle of a horse

Male horses and ponies are called stallions. Females are called mares.

Baby horses and ponies are called foals. A mare is pregnant for about 11 months before giving birth to her foal.

⇧ A foal drinks its mother's milk for about six months.

⇦ A mare licks her foal clean after it is born.

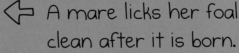

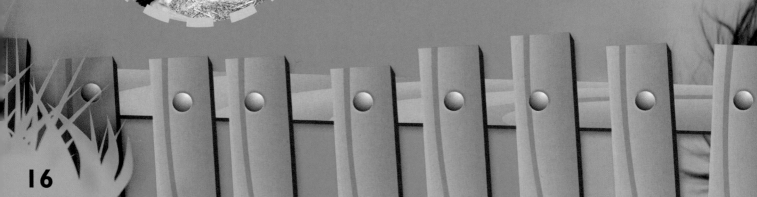

3

⬇ A foal becomes an adult when it is about three years old. Then the life cycle begins again.

Farmyard Fact!

Just like humans, foals are born with no teeth. Their teeth begin to grow when foals are one week old.

Horse and pony breeds

A breed is a type of animal. There are many different breeds of horse and pony.

Fell ponies have short, strong legs. They are used for farm work, such as herding sheep. They can also carry heavy loads, or pull carts.

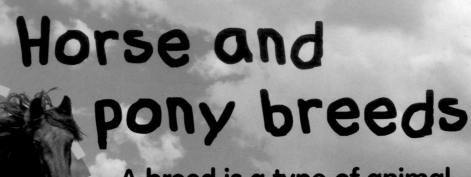

Fell pony

⇧ Most breeds of pony are very strong.

Farmyard Fact!

There are more than 200 different breeds of horse in the world.

Appaloosa horses are used for riding and jumping. They have white, brown or black markings.

The markings on this ⇨ Appaloosa are called 'blanket with spots'.

Quarter horses are common in America, where they work on **cattle ranches**. Quarter horses are very strong and fast.

Cowboys often ride ⇨ quarter horses.

Appaloosa horse

Quarter horse

Hard-working horses

The largest horses are called draught horses. They are hard-working and strong.

Some farmers need draught horses to pull carts and **plough** fields, but most farmers use machines, such as tractors, to do their heavy work.

Draught horses have ⬇ hair around their hooves. This hair is called 'feather'.

harness

Feather

Draught horses are sometimes entered into competitions and horse shows. Their **tack** is covered with decorations made of brass. Their manes and tails are brushed and plaited for horse shows.

⇧ Draught horses have large heads and strong necks.

Farmyard Fact!

Draught horses can be more than 180 centimetres (18 hands) tall. That's as tall as an adult man!

Glossary

Bridle
This is used to control a horse. A bridle is made of leather straps and the reins are attached to it.

Cattle
Cows, bulls and calves are collectively known as cattle.

Cowboy
A person who rides horses on a cattle ranch is called a cowboy or cowgirl.

Farrier
Farriers are people who look after horses' hooves and fit their shoes.

Graze
When an animal feeds on grass in fields it is said to be grazing.

Markings
Some horses and ponies have patches of colour on their fur. These are called markings.

Mucking out
When someone cleans a stable they are mucking out.

Plough
Farmers have to plough, or turn the soil over, before they can plant their seeds. They use a plough to do this job.

Ranch
A ranch is a very large farm.

Tack
Stirrups, reins, bridles and saddles are all called tack.

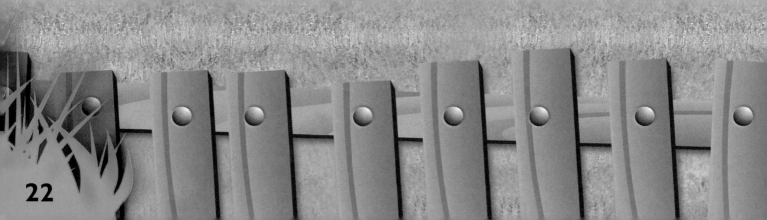

Index

Notes for parents and teachers

 Look through the book together, talk about the pictures, and find new words in the Glossary.

It is fun to find ways that animals are similar, or different to one another – and observing these things is a core science skill. Children could draw pictures of animals with four legs, or ones that eat plants, for example, and go on to identify those that are both plant-eaters and four-legged.

 Talk about the basic needs that animals and humans share, such as food, space and shelter. Encourage the child to think about how wild animals get their food and find shelter.

 Encourage children to learn more about horses by researching different breeds of horse on the Internet, or by going to a local stable or farm.